Original title:
The Language of Accessories

Copyright © 2025 Creative Arts Management OÜ
All rights reserved.

Author: Isaac Ravenscroft
ISBN HARDBACK: 978-1-80586-047-1
ISBN PAPERBACK: 978-1-80586-519-3

Palette of Personality

A scarf can sing in vibrant hues,
While hats gossip with playful views.
A belt that jokes with a trusty clasp,
Shoes that dance, forever grasp.

Woven Narratives

Earrings tell tales of wild nights,
Bracelets wink under city lights.
A woven bag, a riddle in thread,
Socks with stripes, oh what a spread!

Trinkets of Time

Watches tick with a cheeky grin,
Rings whisper secrets of where you've been.
A necklace that jests with every swing,
Time is a player—wear it like bling!

Statements in Stone

Rings of stone make sarcastic claims,
Cuffs that chuckle at boring names.
A pendant laughing at the day's dull grind,
In every gem, a jest you'll find.

Dialogue in Design

A hat that tilts with style so bold,
Whispers secrets that never grow old.
Scarves that swirl in colors bright,
Giggle at life with sheer delight.

Earrings that jingle like laughter's song,
Chasing the beat where we all belong.
Rings that spin with a playful twist,
Dreams wrapped up in a fashionable mist.

Interwoven Tales

A belt that holds stories untold,
Tales of fashion, both new and old.
Socks with stripes that dance in pairs,
Tickling toes and igniting stares.

Brooches that wink and nod with flair,
Committing crimes on the dull and bare.
Gloves that plot to match and clash,
Creating drama with a glamorous splash.

Statements of Stitches

A patchwork bag with patterns divine,
Looks like a quilt, but ain't it fine?
Buttons that boast with a cheeky grin,
Each one hoping for a wild spin.

Threads that tangle like secrets spun,
In the dance of fabric, there's always fun.
Pockets that joke about hidden dreams,
Sewing smiles with their crafty schemes.

Glamour's Grammar

Necklaces that chatter and twist with glee,
Teaching us how to accessorize free.
Watches that tick with a chuckle or two,
Timing the moments we all pursue.

Hats that brag about sunny days,
Charming skies with whimsical ways.
Footwear that struts like a comic show,
Learning the rhythm of fashion's flow.

Crafting Comfort

A hat that winks, a scarf that hums,
Bright shoes that dance, oh how they strum!
Bags with sass, belts that chat,
Earrings giggle, isn't that where it's at?

Socks that shake, with stripes so bold,
A brooch that jokes, a story untold!
Gloves that tickle, like an old friend,
This fun ensemble, on trends we depend!

Necklaces wink, with a twinkle or two,
Rings that spin, like they're in a zoo!
A watch that laughs, when late we appear,
Fashion's a joke, we can't help but cheer!

So grab your gear, let's frolic and play,
Each piece a pun, in a quirky display!
Style's a riddle, oh what a blast,
With each accessory, we're having a blast!

Textured Translations

Beads that chatter, bangles that jive,
A cape that flutters, oh it's alive!
Crazy glasses, with colors that clash,
Each item a punchline, bringing a laugh!

A tie that twists, with a wink on the end,
Shoes with attitude, they walk and blend!
A quirky hat that teases the eyes,
Watch it sway, like it's got its own size!

Cuffs that snicker, with every twist,
Brooches that dance, oh don't they insist?
A purse that's sassy, with lips in a pout,
When fashion calls, you better shout out!

These playful layers, they tell a tale,
With each little piece, we're sure to prevail!
So mix and match, let your joy unfurl,
In the silly world of style, let's give it a whirl!

Gems That Speak

Rings that twinkle, gossip in light,
Earrings chuckle, all through the night.
Brooches share tales, fashionably bold,
While bracelets wink secrets, never to scold.

Necklaces prattle, draping with flair,
A watch rolls its eyes, with time to spare.
In this chatter, gems jive with glee,
Wearing your joy, so effortlessly.

Fashioned Voices

Scarves wave hello with a whimsical twirl,
Hats tip and nod, giving smiles a whirl.
Belts cinch the laughter, snug as a hug,
While socks make puns, cozy and smug.

Shoes click and clack, dancing through air,
With every step, they spread joy to share.
The buttons keep secrets, stitched with a grin,
While pockets hold giggles tucked softly within.

Emblems of Emotion

A pin that winks, a splash of delight,
Sunglasses shield laughter, day into night.
Watches tick-tock with jokes in the gears,
While ties rattle tales, fueling the cheers.

Clutches hold whispers, secrets so sly,
Headbands sashay with a sassy reply.
Each piece a character, quirky and bright,
In this fashion play, joy takes its flight.

Silhouettes of Sentiment

Charming charms jingle, in playful parade,
While cuffs crack up in a fashionable charade.
Totes tell a story, hefty with glee,
Silhouettes strut with sheer jubilee.

Patches provide punchlines, sewn with a wink,
And slippers giggle when you're on the brink.
Every accessory beams with a grin,
In this colorful world, it's fun to begin.

The Fabric of Identity

In a world of zippers and flair,
My socks tell stories, if you dare.
Bowties giggle, they dance around,
While hats nod secrets, oh so profound.

Scarves wrap jokes, snug and tight,
Sandals squeak in pure delight.
Belt buckles wink, with a flick,
Each piece whispers: life's a trick!

Expressions in Fabric

A shirt with stripes and wild hues,
Makes serious moments just a ruse.
Pants that promise comfort and laughs,
Jokes unfold in pleats and drafts.

The fashion world, a jesters' stage,
Where sweatshirts scream, 'Turn the page!'
With every button, a chuckle's glean,
In threads, we find the humor unseen.

Brooches of Belief

A brooch that flaunts a laughing cat,
Speaks louder than a politician's chitchat.
With glittering smiles and absurd shapes,
Each pin a story, as laughter escapes.

Kudos to necklaces that sway and tease,
Dancing around with the greatest of ease.
Accessories, the jesters of our attire,
A sunbeam's joke, never to tire!

The Messages We Wear

Oh, shirts proclaiming, 'I woke up like this,'
Mocking Mondays with a smirking bliss.
Hats that claim, 'I'm just here for snacks,'
Each garment layers laughter, no cracks.

Earrings that jingle, a mischievous tune,
Dance on earlobes, from morn 'til moon.
In this parade of quirky attire,
We wear our chuckles, never to tire!

Tokens of Taste

Bling on the fingers, oh what a sight,
A brooch that sparkles like a disco light.
Socks with stripes that surely clash,
But they make me giggle, oh, what a bash!

A hat too big, it blocks my view,
Flip-flops in winter? Who knew?
Ties that twist, and shoelaces flare,
Each piece a laugh, beyond compare!

Scribbles in Silk

Scarves that swirl like a mad dance,
Hats that ask, "Do you dare take a chance?"
Bows that bounce on heads with glee,
Fashion's a joke, just look at me!

A tie-dye shirt with colors so bold,
Pants that tell stories, yet to be told.
Mix and match? Oh, what a game,
Each quirky piece has its own claim to fame!

The Signature of Style

Do socks need flair? Oh yes, indeed!
With polka dots dancing, they take the lead.
A jacket that clashes, but still feels right,
Bringing smiles with every quirky sight.

Shoes that chirp with each little step,
A belt that squeaks, making me prep.
Style isn't serious; it's a fun parade,
With giggles and charm, fashion's been made!

Threads of Tradition

Grandma's pearls, a history told,
Worn with jeans, breaking the mold.
A waistcoat spotted with vibrant flair,
Traditions twisted in laughter we share.

Kimonos spin with a playful whirl,
Lifting spirits, giving life a twirl.
Each stitch a story, a chuckle or two,
In the fabric of life, we're wrapped in the hue!

The Poetry of Pearls

In a string of pearls, a tale is spun,
Each round little ball, a little bit fun.
They dance on necks like a waltzy pair,
Winking at foes with a delicate glare.

Oh, the way they clatter, a gossip in tow,
Whispers of elegance, but watch them glow!
With every clink, a new giggle starts,
Adorning the necks of wild, wacky hearts.

Sentiments in Scarves

Twirled up in knots, a colorful flair,
Scarves are the stories that float in the air.
Every wrap whispers a stylish decree,
Fashion's soft blanket, a joke for the free.

From polka dots bold to stripes that amaze,
Each choice a giggle that sets us ablaze.
They swish and they sway in a fabric parade,
Knitted with laughter, never afraid.

Tokens of Identity

Brooches and pins, a quirky array,
Tell secrets of wearers, in a comical way.
A cat or a cupcake, a statement of pride,
Sitting on jackets like they're on a ride.

Each piece is a word in a silly charade,
A treasure of laughter, so brightly displayed.
A flamingo that winks or a taco that smiles,
Tokens for all in their whimsical styles.

Glistening Stories

Bracelets that jingle, a merry old tune,
Sparkles and shimmers that capture the moon.
They chatter like friends whenever they shine,
Each bead a confetti of laughter divine.

Rings that twist tales in circles so grand,
Stacked like opinions that boldly withstand.
With every glimmer, a punchline is found,
Crafting bright moments, joy tightly wound.

Whispers of the Wardrobe

Bangles jingle like a cat's purr,
Hats whisper secrets, soft and blurred.
Scarves twirl tales of blustery days,
While shoes tap dance in playful ways.

Collars and cuffs like chatty friends,
Debating fashion, setting trends.
In pockets, laughter finds a place,
A missing sock, a funny face!

The Poem of Patterns

Polka dots play peek-a-boo,
Stripes argue, 'No, I'm better than you!'
Floral prints throw a garden party,
And plaid just hopes to look hearty.

Checks check in with a clever grin,
As paisley claims it's the best to win.
Gingham giggles at the whole affair,
While tie-dye spins in colorful flair.

Subtle Signs of Significance

A tiny pin on a lapel's tale,
Speaks of journeys, quirky and pale.
Bracelets charm in whispered tones,
Sharing secrets like ancient stones.

Earrings dangle, gossip in flight,
While a brooch winks, 'Isn't this bright?'
Each trinket tells a tale so sly,
A wink and nod from fabric nigh.

The Timelessness of Touch

A velvet scarf feels like a dream,
While silk ties shimmer, make hearts beam.
Woolen hats cocoon winter's chill,
And leather gloves give a classy thrill.

Rings of all sizes give sweet smiles,
Creating memories across the miles.
A belt's embrace—comfort and cheer,
As socks declare, 'We're cozy here!'

Echoes of Elegance

A brooch that winks in the light,
Tells tales of fashion, quite a sight.
With each flicker, it plays a game,
Proclaiming loudly, "Look at my fame!"

Earrings dangle and sway with flair,
Whispers of gossip float in the air.
"Did you see? She wears fringe!" they say,
A party for jewels, hip hip hooray!

Trinkets of Identity

A necklace hugs like a long-lost friend,
With charms that giggle, they never end.
"Oh, what stories!" the bracelet cries,
As it sparkles tales from years gone by.

A watch ticks loudly, it joins the fun,
To show off moments, it's second to none.
Hands wave as if saying goodbye,
While rings dance lightly, oh my, oh my!

Stories Woven in Gold

A ring spins tales of lovesick sighs,
While shimmering cuffs throw playful lies.
"I'm the star of this dramatic play!"
Says each shiny piece in a grand array.

Chains jingle with every tiny move,
Crafting a groove that makes you groove.
Laughter erupts from each little gem,
Singing a tune—let's go again!

Conversations in Color

Scarves twist tales in vibrant hues,
Spewing secrets in all the blues.
"I'm the life of this dull shindig!"
A sock declares, sporting a bright wig.

Watches brag with a tick and a tock,
While pins sashay like a royal flock.
Every accessory throws up its hands,
Claiming loud that life's full of bands!

Lustrous Lexicon

A necklace sways, a silent shout,
Telling tales without a doubt.
Earrings dangle like playful charms,
Whispering secrets with their arms.

Rings that twinkle in the sun,
Instantly, style rerun.
Each gem a gossip, so delightfully bright,
A sparkle's language, bold and light.

Words Woven in Wool

Scarves that twist and giggle so,
Wraps of warmth in winter's glow.
Fringes flapping, jokes they share,
A knit or purl, no need to spare.

Sweaters chat, they hug you tight,
In every stitch, a story's flight.
Colors clash in a woolly dance,
Who knew yarn could hold such romance?

Cuffs of Character

Wristbands jingle with a thrill,
Each a promise, a fashion skill.
Colors clash, they raise a cheer,
   Pushing limits, never fear.

Silver chains, like laughter loud,
  In every twist, a playful crowd.
Bangles frolic, around they spin,
Accessories sing; let the fun begin!

The Heartbeats of Handbags

Bags that giggle, with zippers that tease,
Hiding treasures, always at ease.
A tote that whispers silly friends,
In every pocket, the joy never ends.

Clutches that wink at the gala night,
Strutting their stuff, what a sight!
Shopping carts or posh designer flair,
Every handbag holds its secret affair.

Style as Storytelling

A hat with flair, a tale to tell,
Each button's wink casts a spell.
Scarves that whisper, shoes that dance,
Every piece gives fashion a chance.

Earrings chuckle, rings take flight,
A necklace glimmers in the light.
Socks that giggle as you stride,
In this world, accessories guide.

The Allure of Artifacts

A brooch that winks with playful glee,
Each accessory holds a secret spree.
Bracelets jingle, voices all around,
In this charm, laughter's found.

A handbag winks, it knows the way,
To make the mundane seem like play.
A quirky watch that tells no time,
In this circus, style will prime.

Shadows of Chic

Sunglasses strut, they hide and peek,
Obscuring thoughts, they're oh so sleek.
A belt that tightens, a funny squeeze,
Makes you giggle, yet feel at ease.

A bow tie blooms with humor bright,
While hats cap off the jesting night.
Each layer whispers whimsy aside,
In shadows of chic where jokes abide.

Signature Statements

A quirky pin to turn the heads,
Statements whispered with each thread.
Gloves that tease with every clasp,
In the outfit, laughter's grasp.

A funky ring, a playful twist,
To every outfit, joy can't be missed.
From shiny mocks to playful tags,
With every piece, the humor brags.

Charms of Connection

A bracelet here, a ring so bright,
Telling tales of day and night.
Mismatched socks, a funky tie,
Who knew fashion could fly high?

With every pin and every brooch,
We laugh at style, our quirky coach.
A scarf that's polka-dotted blue,
Screams, "I'm fabulous! How 'bout you?"

A button lost, a hat misplaced,
Fashion mishaps, yet we're all graced.
Strutting bold in sandals two-tone,
In this circus, we're never alone.

Silhouettes of Style

A wig that sparkles, shines so bright,
Worn backwards—oh what a sight!
Sunglasses on, indoors they stay,
Who needs sun? It's a fashion play!

A tutu here, some mismatched shoes,
Doing the cha-cha, we just can't lose.
A cape of feathers, who could resist?
In our outfit, we feel like a twist!

The belt's too tight, but who really cares?
We juggle styles like circus bears.
With every quirk, we find our way,
In silhouettes of style, we dance and sway.

The Art of Adornment

A necklace made of pasta and cheese,
Strutting 'round like it's a breeze.
Earrings shaped like tiny fries,
Fashion's meant for laughs and sighs.

The tie's a fish, the shirt a mess,
In this art, we won't digress.
A printed cap that says, "I'm wild!"
With every piece, we're fashion's child.

Bangles clink like joyful chimes,
Dancing to our silly rhymes.
In every gem, a giggle's found,
The art of fun is all around!

Ornaments of Memory

A locket holds my favorite snack,
With gummy bears—what's not to lack?
A charm from Paris, or was it Rome?
Every piece feels like a home.

A belt that squeaks—a secret tune,
Whispering tales beneath the moon.
The brooch I wear, it's grandma's hat,
Telling stories—can you imagine that?

These ornaments, they carry laughs,
In every scratch, in every gaff.
We wear our memories with some flair,
In our hearts, they're always there.

Whispers of Fabric

A scarf that flutters, loud in a breeze,
Whispers of color, aiming to please.
It dodges the ketchup, it drapes with a flair,
Socks in the sandals? A bold fashion dare.

A hat that declares, 'I'm clearly the star,'
With feathers and sequins, it's raising the bar.
The belt's doing yoga, it's cinching so tight,
While earrings are giggling, out shining the night.

Echoes of Elegance

Shoes that squeak secrets on polished floors,
A tale of confidence, each step it endores.
While ties twist and twirl, like dancers in line,
Witty remarks hidden in a pocket in time.

A bracelet that jingles with stories to tell,
Just clink and you'll summon the party's spell.
With charms that are cheeky, and bangles that sway,
Who knew such small things could bring such a play?

Threads of Expression

A shirt with a slogan, bold and absurd,
Puns and odd quirks fly, not a single word blurred.
Pockets for secrets, or maybe just snacks,
The outfit's a puzzle, with tricky knickknacks.

Glasses with flair, both stylish and wide,
Reflecting the laughter we all try to hide.
While hats with a twist say, 'Hello, I'm here!'
In a world made of fabric, joy is quite clear.

Adornments in Silence

A brooch made of glitter, a wink in the light,
Stealing the show, oh what a sight!
With clips that are snappy and pins that can poke,
Accessories chatter, though none of them spoke.

Wristbands that laugh with each flick of the wrist,
Telling the world, 'Oh, don't be dismissed!'
With a wink from a necklace, a friendship unwinds,
In this silent parade, hilarity finds.

Worn Words

A hat tipped low, secrets it keeps,
Whispers of laughter while the world sleeps.
Gloves that clack like gossip machines,
Tell tales of love in vibrant sheens.

A belt that argues, pulling you tight,
Says, "Loose is not cute, get your fit right!"
Socks with stripes, they dance with a twirl,
Each step they take, a story to unfurl.

Scarves that choke, or float in the breeze,
Banter with breezy, carefree ease.
Shoes that squeak with every quick step,
Warning of mischief, the promise of pep.

Earrings jive, a jangling delight,
Chiming along with the mood of the night.
Each piece a tale, a whimsical game,
In a world of quirks, nothing's the same.

The Narrative of Neckties

Neckties dangle, a colorful bunch,
Some are bold, while others just hunch.
A twisty knot, a wobbly friend,
Holds all the gossip that fashion can send.

Polka dots clash with a striped shirt's flair,
A silent feud, but nobody's aware.
In boardroom battles, they wage their war,
Against stuffy collars that we all abhor.

A bow tie giggles, all fancy and neat,
Hoping to charm, not just look sweet.
"I'm quirky!" it cries, while others just frown,
With a playful spirit, it twirls in the town.

The necktie's whisper, a knot of jest,
Each fabric holds tales of every conquest.
In the realm of dress-up, they're kings of the game,
With each little knot, they play for fame.

Expressions in Embellishments

A brooch that winks, with rhinestones aglow,
Pins down the gossip, puts on a show.
Bracelets that rattle, like a crowd at a fair,
They jingle and jangle without a care.

Rings that promise, with their shiny displays,
"I'm fancy!" they boast in the best kind of ways.
Ankle bracelets pull at one's feet with glee,
Dancing around like they just want to be free.

A flashy necklace, bold and grand,
Dripping with stories from a distant land.
Loud as a bell, it demands a reply,
Drawing all eyes as you walk by.

Embellishments chatter, in glittering tones,
Each loaded with laughter, not just with stones.
In this playful realm of wardrobe delight,
They spark wild tales that echo through night.

Crafting a Narrative

A cape that billows, a hero in sight,
Saves the day, with its fabric so bright.
But watch it flutter when the wind decides,
Turning a wonder into a wild ride.

A fanny pack laughs, holding snacks and tales,
Lugging around all the life that prevails.
"I'm handy!" it brags, with pockets galore,
While keeping your treasures, it's never a bore.

A chic headband, with its spunky flair,
Claims to tame curls, like a fashionaire.
Yet when it slips, like a mood gone wrong,
It sings a sweet tune of "What's been so long?"

Crafting a tale with each quirky piece,
In closet chaos, we find our release.
So gather your treasures, and have a good spin,
For fashion's a story, just waiting to begin.

Cuffs and Conversations

Cuffs clasp tight, a wink and a smile,
They gossip and giggle, all the while.
Wristbands jive, a social delight,
Together they dance, all through the night.

Bangles chatter, a clink and a clang,
They tell silly tales that make us all fang.
Bracelets compete for the most flair,
Who knew they'd scheme with such playful care?

The Unseen Dialogue

In pockets they dwell, secrets abound,
Buttons and zippers keep whispers profound.
Handbags throw shade, with a faux pas glance,
Shoes join the fray, urging us to dance.

Scarves swirl around like a playful tease,
Their winks and slick moves put us at ease.
Each stitch a story, each thread a jest,
In this silent chatter, we find our best.

Embellishments of Emotion

Necklaces shimmer, they sparkle in jest,
Each pendant a punchline, bringing out zest.
Earrings dangle low, eavesdropping near,
They giggle and sway, nothing to fear.

Rings are flirty, spinning in fun,
Their shine is a riddle, who's number one?
Chains clink and clatter, a merry brigade,
In this trinket chat, we feel unafraid.

Companions of Charm

Hats tip their brims, as if to confide,
In the world of fashion, they're filled with pride.
Socks slide and giggle, with patterns galore,
They march in a line, always wanting more.

Ties twist and turn, with stories to share,
Their knotty humor fills the most air.
Each accessory whispers, unique in their part,
Crafting a symphony of wearable art.

The Heart of Artistry

A brooch that winks, a scarf that flirts,
Shimmering earrings, all the fun it spurs.
With every clasp, a giggle's found,
In playful hues, our joys abound.

Lace and glitter, colors clashing,
Fashion crimes leave us laughing.
Each accessory, a cheeky jest,
A necklace daring, put to the test.

Forget the rules, let chaos reign,
In layered bracelets, there's no shame.
Our hearts wear twinkles, as we parade,
Crafting smiles, our laughter's made.

In a world of flair, we shine so bright,
Every whimsy piece, a pure delight.
With a wink, we wear our art,
Embracing love, and quirky heart.

Accessories as Allies

A hat that's jaunty, a belt that teases,
Helping us to conquer, with effortless breezes.
Our loyal rings, whispering style,
And quirky pins that make us smile.

With funky socks and shoes that squeak,
Each playful piece, our personality speaks.
Tie a bow, let's celebrate cheer,
Accessories always are near and dear.

In mismatched glory, we strut about,
Laughing loud, letting worries out.
Our true selves shine, no need to disguise,
With twirls and turns, we claim the skies.

So here's to our partners, our trusty friend,
In fashion's chaos, we gladly blend.
The world's our stage, let's give a cheer,
For the playful pieces we hold so dear.

Voices of Vanity

Stilettos talk, they make us tall,
Whispers of glitter, echoing through the hall.
With every step, a giggle lies,
In fashion's game, there's no disguise.

A clutch that clinks, it's fashion's tune,
Sassy shades, strutting under the moon.
Hats that shimmy, bows that shout,
In our kingdom of quirks, we dance about.

We're a colorful bunch, a vibrant mix,
Competing laughter, our trickster fix.
Each outfit speaks, loud as a drum,
In the whirly world, we call it fun.

Though cheeks may ache from all our grins,
Fashion's our playground, let the fun begin!
We raise our glasses, fashion's our song,
In the chorus of laughter, we all belong.

The Celebration of Curves

Ribbons that sway, and beads that bounce,
Making heads turn, and hearts arouse.
Fashion's a party, come one, come all,
Each curve celebrated, we stand tall.

With sassy belts hugging tight,
Shapes in motion, oh what a sight!
Jingling bangles, a festive tune,
Our silhouettes dance, like flowers in bloom.

Strutting wide, from side to side,
Each accessory a ride on joy's tide.
A flutter of lace, a playful wink,
In this joyous romp, we never sink.

So gather 'round, let's raise a cheer,
To all the curves that bring us near.
With flair and laughter, we take the stage,
Celebrating uniqueness, at every age!

Prestige of Patterns

In polka dots, I take my stand,
A plaid shirt says, "I'm so unplanned!"
Stripes declare my fashion fight,
While checks leave all my style in sight.

A floral tie, oh what's that flair!
Bows and beads, I must declare.
My socks are loud, they dance around,
In this style circus, I'm profound!

Lace-up shoes with neon dreams,
Funky hats echo silly themes.
With each piece, I strut and sway,
Making fashion wild in every way.

From slip-ons to the chunky heels,
Accessory games give all the feels.
With colors bright, I rule the scene,
In this mad world, I reign supreme!

Tokens of Time

My watch ticks loudly, time in a brawl,
Digital or analog, it's all my call.
With each tick-tock, I strut with glee,
Fashionably late, just like me!

A pocket square, such a fancy sight,
Using tools of the trade just feels so right.
Old-fashioned glasses topped with flair,
I see the world through a stylish glare.

A bracelet jingles, sings my tune,
While rings do dance beneath the moon.
Each minute matters, or so they say,
But I'm too busy to care today!

With pendants that dangle, they cheer and tease,
Wristwatches whisper, "Catch us, please!"
In this world of ticks and turns,
Style and laughter, my heart still yearns!

Accessories as Art

Brooches glitter like stars at night,
On jackets, they spark a joyful light.
I wear a canvas, my body, my show,
With arms adorned, watch the colors flow!

Earrings sway, they bob and dip,
In every movement, they play and flip.
Necklaces laugh, as they twist and twine,
Each piece a tale, every loop a line.

Scarves tell stories of trips and dreams,
In windswept colors, my heart still gleams.
With quirky styles that challenge the norm,
I twirl and whirl in this vibrant storm.

In the gallery of my closet, they hide,
A joyful collection, my art and pride.
Dressing up, I'm the masterpiece,
With laughter and flair, my love will increase!

Signals of Sophistication

A fedora tipped, what's that? A cue!
With shades so dark, I'm incognito too.
A belt so bold, it cinches with flair,
In the game of style, I ride on air.

Chic gloves clapping, they join the fun,
While scarves in the breeze declare I've won.
Shoes that shimmer, stealing the scene,
Making every step feel like a dream.

Purses boast of secrets untold,
With textures and colors bright and bold.
Each accessory whispers, "Look at me!"
In this stylish duel, I glide so free.

Every piece, a pondered thought,
My outfit's scream can't be bought.
With playful wit, I dazzle and twirl,
In a world where fashion's a merry whirl!

Shapes of Sentiment

A hat that shouts, "I'm quirky!"
Socks with polka dots and glee.
Each button tells a little tale,
In fabric worlds, we laugh and sail.

Shoes that squeak, a jolly tune,
Belts that twist like a cartoon.
A scarf that winks in vibrant hues,
Fashion's fun when it plays blues.

Glasses large, like bug-eyed dreams,
Earrings swing with silly screams.
A belt so bright it steals the show,
In this array, let giggles flow.

A brooch that looks like cheese and wine,
Adds a twist that's so divine.
In jumbles of style, we find our place,
Accessories hold a warm embrace.

The Dialect of Drapery

A tie that dances with every move,
A cape that makes you want to groove.
Cuffs that chime like little bells,
In every fold, a story tells.

A belt that thinks it's part of art,
Pockets with secrets to impart.
Bandanas waving in the breeze,
Fashion whispers, "Do as you please!"

Sweaters sporting goofy prints,
Add a quirky zing like mints.
A coat that flares with bold delight,
Turning drab into a joyous sight.

In mismatched styles, joy's the key,
Each piece a note in harmony.
Through drapery soft, laughter flows,
It's whimsy that the heart bestows.

Adorned Whispers

A necklace hums a secret tune,
Rings that twinkle like the moon.
Brooches gossip, gems in line,
In splendid style, friends align.

A bracelet that ticks with playful cheer,
Hats that tip, always near.
Scarves that flutter, a breeze of flair,
Adornments laughing, unaware.

With every clasp, a story swaps,
In funky styles, our laughter hops.
A quirky piece upon my head,
In silly style, the world's misled.

Funky glasses with polka dots,
Bringing giggles, tying knots.
Through whispers soft, our smiles reign,
Adorned tales, we share the gain.

Threads of Silence

A jacket grins with patchy pride,
Suspenders dance and never hide.
Pants that swish like playful fish,
In style's embrace, we find our wish.

A pocket square with vibrant flair,
Winks and nods, a sight to share.
Socks that poke out, colors bright,
With every step, we giggle light.

Caps that tilt with cheeky curls,
Layers of laughter, twirls and swirls.
In stitches neat, a chuckle grows,
Threaded stories, joy bestows.

Through fabric's charm, we spin and twist,
Finding humor in what's missed.
In threads so bold, our voices hum,
A tapestry of laughs, we come.

The Luster of Self-Expression

A funky hat atop my head,
It makes my thoughts run wild, I said.
With every twirl of beads I wear,
I strut like I just don't care!

Socks that clash in bold display,
Are just my style; it's my own way.
Shoes that squeak with every step,
Kind of like I'm on a rep!

From oversized glasses to blingy rings,
Each piece is more than just some things.
In this colorful, silly dance,
I cheerfully invite you to take a chance!

So let your outfit have a voice,
In sparkles, stripes, make your choice!
For in each thread and color there lies,
The art of laughter, the joy that aligns.

Bracelets of Belonging

My wrist adorned with a clanging crew,
Each charm is weird, but fits just you!
Friendship bands in colors bright,
Silently shouting: 'We're outta sight!'

A rubber ducky, a tiny shoe,
Little bits of crazy, who knew?
They jingle jangle, dance so free,
Telling tales of you and me!

One that glows like a disco ball,
Best worn in the wildest hall.
Together we shine, a motley clash,
Funky wrist-wear in a joyful flash!

So stack 'em high, let's make a rhyme,
With every movement, we take our time.
For in this jolly, playful string,
We find the laughter that bracelets bring.

Necklaces of Narratives

Around my neck, a tale is spun,
A quirky pendant, a silly pun.
A llama charm that's quite absurd,
Whispers loudly without a word!

Each bead a story, bright and clear,
From the jungle or maybe the pier.
A tiny globe showing where I'd roam,
It's like wearing my heart—my own little home!

The longer it hangs, the wiser it grows,
Tell me a secret, that nobody knows.
With knotted string and laughing flair,
My necklace dances—who says it's rare?

So swing it, twist it, show it bright,
Let every neckwear bring delight.
For in this whimsy we find our place,
In tales and trinkets, we share a space.

Echoing Statements

A brooch shaped like a silly fish,
"Catch me if you can!" is my only wish.
With every glance, it journeys far,
Wink and wave, my starry czar!

A colorful pin with a cheeky grin,
Says it all with a little spin.
Expressing dreams, from dusk till dawn,
Who knew fashion could carry on?

Earrings that sway with every laugh,
Conversations weave a vibrant path.
These small details spark the fun,
Worn like crowns—each one a pun!

So speak with flair, let style be bold,
In shiny whispers, our stories told.
For in this jive, we all unite,
In a world of accessories that feel just right.

Accessories in Verses

A hat that's always in the way,
It bounces back with every sway.
Sunglasses smile on the nose,
They hide the truth, but who even knows?

A scarf that twirls like it's on a quest,
It ties itself, it knows no rest.
Bracelets jingle with a cheeky laugh,
They share secrets, do the math!

Rings that twist and spin around,
They argue who wears the crown.
Bags that whisper in a jive,
"Look at me! I'm quite alive!"

Shoes that dance without a beat,
They stomp and skip, they think they're fleet.
With every step, they throw a show,
Oh, the drama, here we go!

The Soft Speak of Suede

Suede shoes talk with a quiet flair,
They softly tread, as if on air.
They whisper tales from days gone by,
Dodging puddles, oh so spry!

A bag of suede, all plush and neat,
It tells a story with every seat.
With tiny pockets, it wears a grin,
"Oh, darling, come on, let's go in!"

Cushioned layers, they make a scene,
Babbling soft, they're so serene.
In playful nudges, they conjure glee,
Oh suede, you're wild, just let it be!

Engraved Emotions

A pendant whispers sweet and low,
It carries tales that ebb and flow.
Each little scratch, a memory kept,
In this jewelry box, secrets leapt.

Rings etched with giggles, bright as can be,
"Hold on tight, we're a jolly spree!"
Charm bracelets rattle with every jest,
They keep the spirit of fun at best.

Lockets clasped with sighs and dreams,
They hold indoors all the moonbeams.
With every gaze, they wink and smirk,
These engraved trinkets, oh the perks!

Identity in Adornment

A flashy watch that claims the time,
It boasts in bling, how truly sublime!
Tiny charms that giggle and sway,
"Oh look at me, don't look away!"

Necklaces like ribbons on a gift,
Each twinkling bead gives a little lift.
Brooches wink, in a cheeky chat,
Saying "Darling, here's where it's at!"

Earrings that sway, they dance in air,
They flirt with breezes, without a care.
In every piece, a joke is spun,
Identity blooms, we're here for fun!

A Tapestry of Touch

A bracelet jangles with glee,
Quirky charms dance, wild and free.
Earrings like giggles, swaying bright,
Whispering secrets in the night.

Hats that tip and wink at you,
Scarves that twirl in colors true.
Belt buckles chuckle, make us grin,
Each accessory whispers, 'Come join in!'

Socks with patterns, so bizarre,
Tell tales of places near and far.
Shoes that squeak with every step,
Invite a laugh, a joyful pep.

So gather 'round, let's have some fun,
With trinkets shining in the sun.
For every piece has quite a tale,
And laughter hides in every detail.

The Subtlety of Sparkle

A necklace winks from across the room,
Its shimmer makes the dullness bloom.
Rings that giggle, fingers in tow,
Grinning with bling, putting on a show.

A brooch with sass, looks here and there,
Daring the tie to try and compare.
Gloves that prance like they own the floor,
Bringing pizazz, who could ask for more?

Watches that tick in quirky rhymes,
Counting each laughter, marking good times.
Funky hairpins that play peekaboo,
Crafting a story, just for you.

It's all a game, this playful zest,
With sparkle and shine, we're truly blessed.
Each little gem has a giggle inside,
So wear your joy, let it be your guide.

Dialogue in Designs

A hat that whispers, 'What's the scoop?'
While shoes stamp out their funky troupe.
Belts play coy, their buckles tease,
As jackets shimmy just to please.

Wristbands chatter, making a jest,
'Who wore it better?' they love to quest.
Sunglasses hide winks, oh-so-cool,
In this fashion jungle, who's the fool?

Each accessory has a voice so loud,
Speaking in styles that fashion made proud.
Scarves like poets recite their verse,
Draping around necks, they happily nurse.

So toss on a gem, let the fun begin,
Converse with colors, sparkles, and spin.
In this chatter of treasures, don't hold back,
Join the friendly banter, wear your knack!

Ornaments of the Heart

A charm bracelet jingles, tales to tell,
Of wild adventures and coffee spells.
Keychains giggle, 'We're doorbell-free!'
Unlocking smiles as we roam with glee.

Necklaces share secrets, glistening bright,
Like old pals who chat deep into the night.
Earrings wink, playful and sweet,
Dancing with rhythm, shuffling their feet.

Purses chime in, 'Let's grab a drink!'
Late night treasures make us wink.
A pin on the collar shares a laugh,
Crafting connections, a heartfelt path.

So as you adorn your joyful soul,
Embrace each piece, let laughter roll.
With trinkets close, let your heart soar,
For every ornament dances with joy galore!

Verses of Velvet

In velvet shoes, I strut with flair,
Green and pink, a fashion dare.
My hat's a bird, it chirps all day,
Who knew clothes could laugh and play?

A scarf that glows like neon lights,
Turns heads quicker than fancy fights.
Socks that twirl with a silly glee,
They dance on feet, just wait and see!

My belt's a snake, coiling tight,
With every meal, it puts up a fight.
Gloves that tickle my friends' noses,
Fashion can bring out some funny poses!

Each button's a smile, each stitch a joke,
My wardrobe's a laugh—a colorful poke.
So here's to style, in all its quirks,
Wrap it in humor, that's how it works!

Reflections in Gold

In golden chains, I hear a tingle,
They jingle-jangle, it makes me giggle.
Rings that wiggle on my toes,
Who knew bling could come with prose?

A necklace chimes like playful bells,
It whispers secrets, it shares my spells.
Earrings swing like happy dreams,
A little shine can burst at the seams!

My watch ticks time—oh, what a tease!
Every minute's a chance to squeeze.
Bracelets chatter, they're my best friends,
In this golden game, the fun never ends!

Reflections shine, like laughter's light,
In every glance, they shine so bright.
Jokes in jewels make the day unfold,
Who knew my closet could be such gold?

Language of Layers

A hatstack towers, a lofty show,
Stacked like pancakes, in a row.
Shirts that layer like cake so sweet,
Each slice reveals a different beat!

My coat's a hug, it wraps me tight,
Makes me feel like a fluffy kite.
Underneath, a shirt that's a meme,
Flaunting jokes in a stylish theme!

Socks peek out from shorts so bold,
A fashion faux pas, or so I'm told.
While layers tell tales, which one to choose?
Decisions in fabric, I never lose!

In this layered fun, I find my way,
A fashion puzzle, all in play.
With laughter stitched in every seam,
Here's to my clothes—living the dream!

Statements in Simplicity

A simple tee, yet oh so bright,
It glows like sunshine, pure delight.
Pants that whisper, "Keep it chill,"
No fuss, no frills, just fashion thrill.

My shoes are modest, no flashy flair,
But they certainly take me anywhere.
Wristbands shout in tones of fun,
In simplicity, my style's begun!

A classic cap can say it all,
No need for sparkle or a ball.
With subtle themes, I strut my claim,
In quiet coolness, I play the game!

Simple charms that tickle the mind,
In understated truth, joy you'll find.
So here's to the basics, my playful friends,
In statements that giggle, the fun never ends!

Swaying with Scarves

Scarves drape like playful clouds,
Wrapping necks in whimsical shrouds.
Twists and turns in a colorful dance,
Accentuating outfits with just a glance.

They flutter and sway in the breeze,
Giving plain jackets a touch with ease.
One minute a pirate, the next a queen,
With a flick of the fabric, you're all set to dream.

Dazzling prints and patterns galore,
Confusing folks with patterns they adore.
Tangled in knots, oh what a sight,
Turning heads and hearts with sheer delight.

A scarlet one gives a power boost,
While polka dots spark joy, oh what a hoot!
Bows and twists, they all come to play,
Striding through life in a scarf ballet.

The Intimacy of Accessories

A brooch winks on a lapel with flair,
Whispering secrets as if we care.
Earrings dangle, swinging like chimes,
Chiming in tune with silly rhymes.

Rings that hug fingers, snug and tight,
Making hands feel extra bright.
One sparkles, one makes a silly face,
Creating a charm you can't replace.

Bracelets jangle with every move,
Making heartbeats groove and prove.
They gossip and giggle when you're not aware,
A clinking party, chaos in the air.

Together they whisper, together they shout,
Accessories make the world spin about.
With a wink and a nudge, they bring the cheer,
Turning daily drab into a grand frontier!

Threads of Thought

Threads weave stories in vibrant hues,
Creating laughter with every muse.
A belt that cinches with zany pride,
Holds up dreams that refuse to hide.

A hairpin shaped like a grinning cat,
Teasing the world, "Look at that!"
In a messy bun or a braid so neat,
It adds personality, oh what a treat!

Shoes that squeak with every step,
Creating a symphony where secrets are kept.
Laces bow and twist in a joyful spree,
Making each sidewalk feel like a jubilee.

In this fabric of laughter and fun,
Every thread shouts, "Come join the run!"
With each accessory, our spirits ignite,
Turning drab into fab, oh what a sight!

The Charm of Composition

A necklace here, a pin over there,
Creating a mashup with love to spare.
Like mismatched socks, they play tricks,
Fashioning chaos with daring flicks.

Stacked high with bracelets, a colorful tower,
They scream elegance, oh what power!
Polished stones and quirky charms,
Each piece a secret, disarming alarms.

A floppy hat with flair and fun,
Casting shadows, hiding none.
Draped in style, a walk in the sun,
Accessories make life a wild run.

With each layer, a playful jest,
Adding humor to a daily quest.
In this collage of quirky delight,
We dance through life, hearts feeling light!

Echoes of Embellishment

A hat that shouts, 'Oh please, wear me!'
A brooch that winks, 'Just wait and see!'
Earrings jingle, a playful tune,
Fashion's finest, dancing in June.

Bags that giggle, they've stories to tell,
Scarves that whisper secrets so well.
Shoes that prance, with a cheeky stride,
Every piece, a wild joyride.

The Rhythm of Rings

Rings that dazzle, they spin a tale,
One says 'crazy' and another 'pale'.
Stack them high, what a silly sight,
Like a tower that tips just from one slight.

Fingers twinkle, they jive and sway,
A blingy echo, come join the play!
Knuckles laugh, in a shiny embrace,
Who knew they'd hold, such each other's grace?

Fashioned Whispers

A necklace giggles, dangling bright,
It murmurs softly, 'Oh, what a night!'
Bracelets jangle with glee so loud,
Like a party of jewels, jeweled and proud.

A belt that chuckles, 'Tighter, I dare!'
While shades hide smiles behind their glare.
Purses with winks, naughty and bold,
Accents chatter tales yet untold.

Heartstrings and Handbags

A handbag struts, 'I'm the life of the crowd!'
It's full of secrets, oh so loud!
With pockets that giggle and zippers that hum,
It carries dreams, making all hearts drum.

Crazy hats tip, they're in on the joke,
Funky pins teasing with every poke.
Each accessory, a sprightly friend,
Binding laughter, 'round every bend.'

A Symphony of Style

A hat talks big, it takes the lead,
With feathers and flair, it plants the seed.
Shoes stutter in rhythm, click-clack on the floor,
As they tap dance their way to the sought-after store.

Belts are a hiccup, holding things tight,
While bags gossip secrets, hidden from sight.
Each accessory strums, creating a tune,
In a closet ensemble, they'll dance 'neath the moon.

Charms of Connection

An earring giggles, swinging with cheer,
While bracelets wave hello, bringing you near.
A necklace whispers, a shimmer so grand,
Enticing attention, like it's got a fan.

Rings jingle and jive, keeping the score,
Each piece alive, asking for more.
Together they mingle, crafting a scene,
In this carnival of color, their joy is seen.

The Poetry of Embellishment

Scarves flutter like pages, stories untold,
As they wrap 'round your neck, in colors bold.
Glasses perch high, looking oh-so wise,
But they really just spy on the cute guys.

Pins have a pun, they're never quite plain,
Winking at shirts, causing a chain.
In this quirky rhyme, the layers delight,
Every accessory dancing, in day and night.

Adjectives in Jewelry

Chunky or dainty, each charm has a flair,
Sparkly and sassy, they buzz through the air.
Hoops spin like tales, spinning round with glee,
While studs wink and nod, like 'Come dance with me!'

Colors collide, like a splash fight in spring,
Every piece proclaiming what joy they can bring.
In this whimsical world, laughter is gold,
With trinkets that giggle, let the stories unfold.

www.ingramcontent.com/pod-product-compliance
Lightning Source LLC
Chambersburg PA
CBHW060115230426
43661CB00003B/193